I AM A
lezzie
butch
pervert
girlfriend
bulldagger
sister
dyke
AND PROUD!

fierce pussy

I AM A

stone butch

androgyne

femme

tomboy

girlfriend

sapphic

deviant

AND PROUD

fierce pussy

I AM A
mannish
muffdiver
amazon
feminist
queer
lesbian
femme
AND PROUD!

fierce pussy

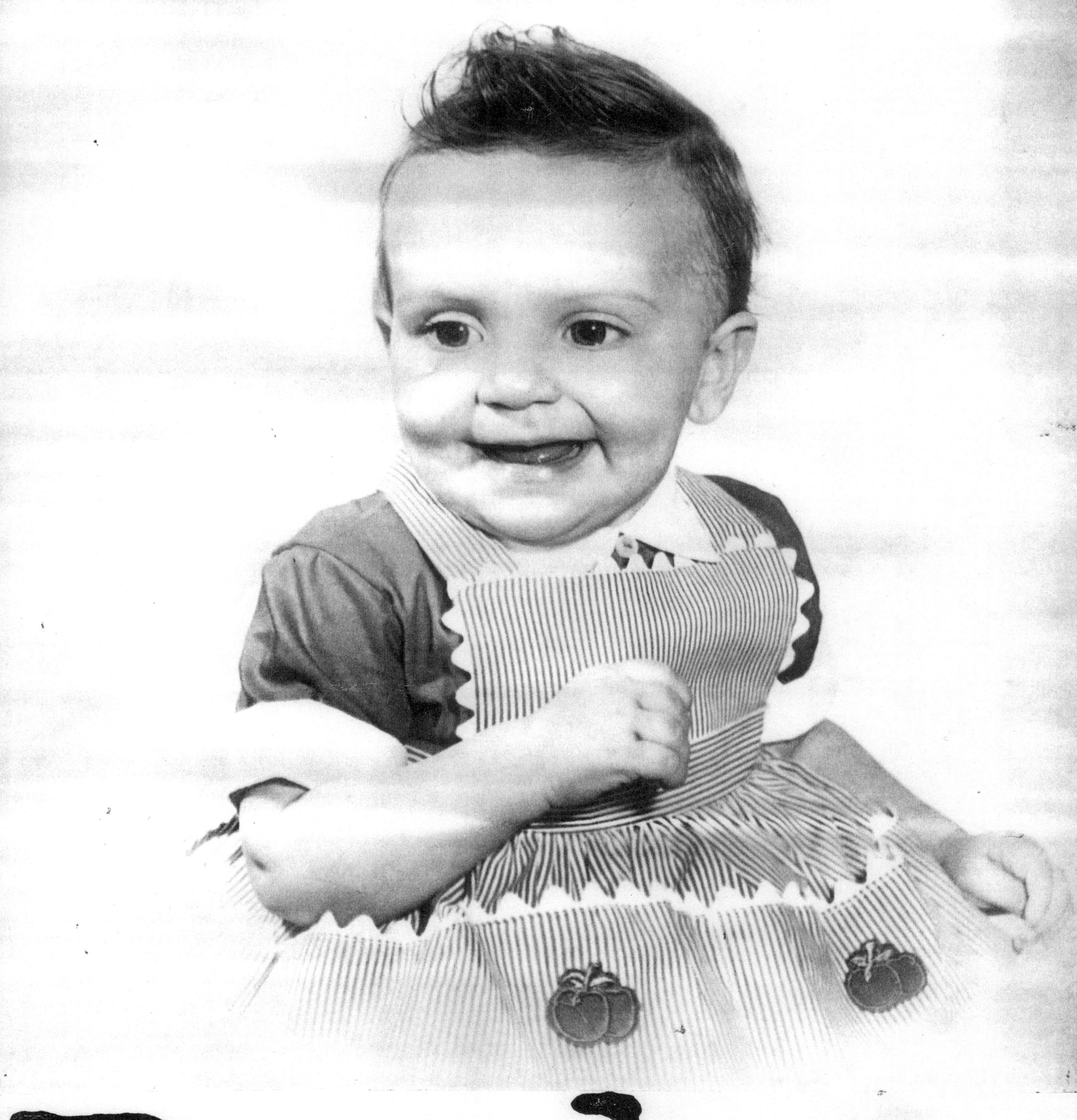

Dyke

fierce pussy

lesbian

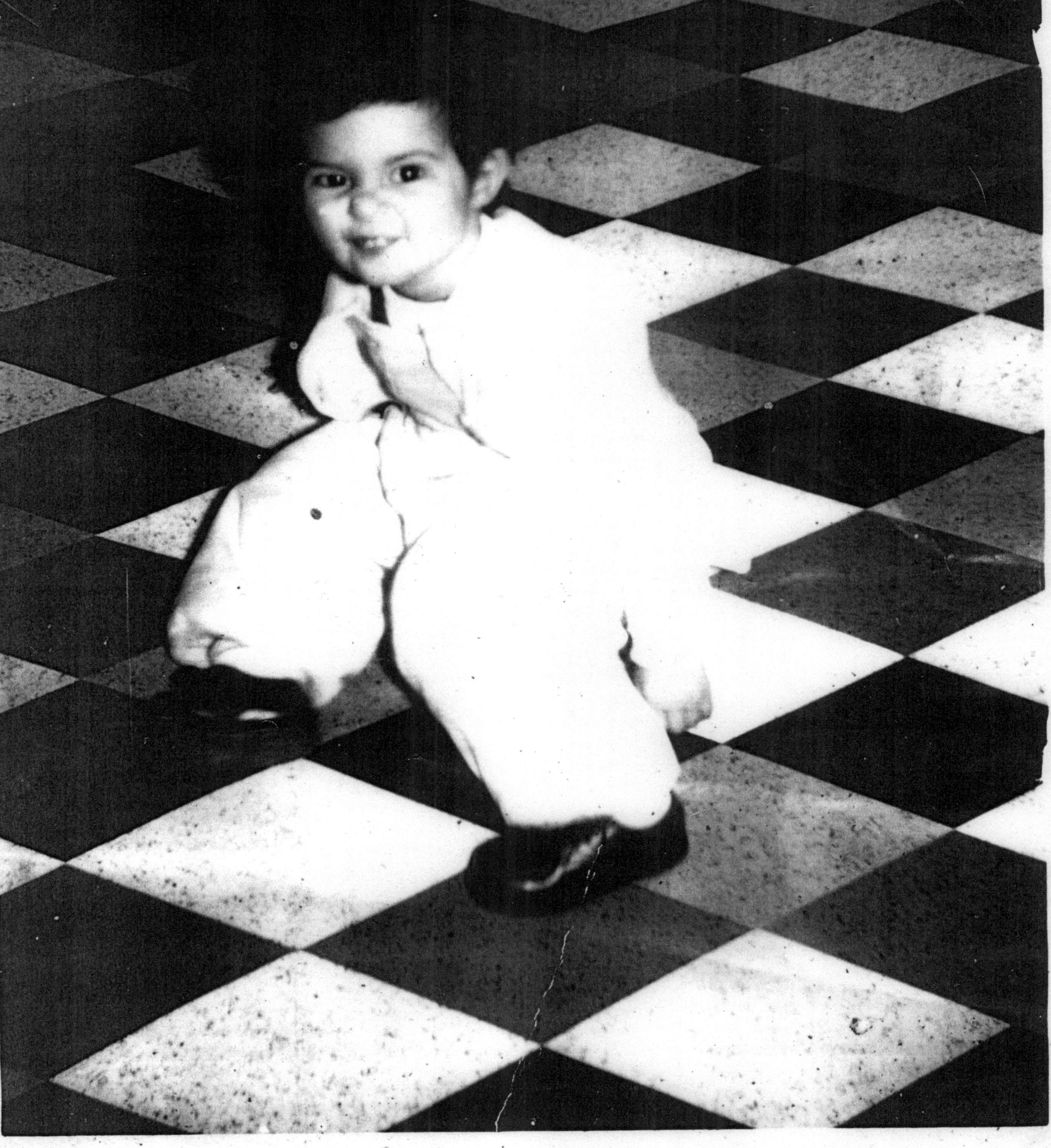

fierce pussy

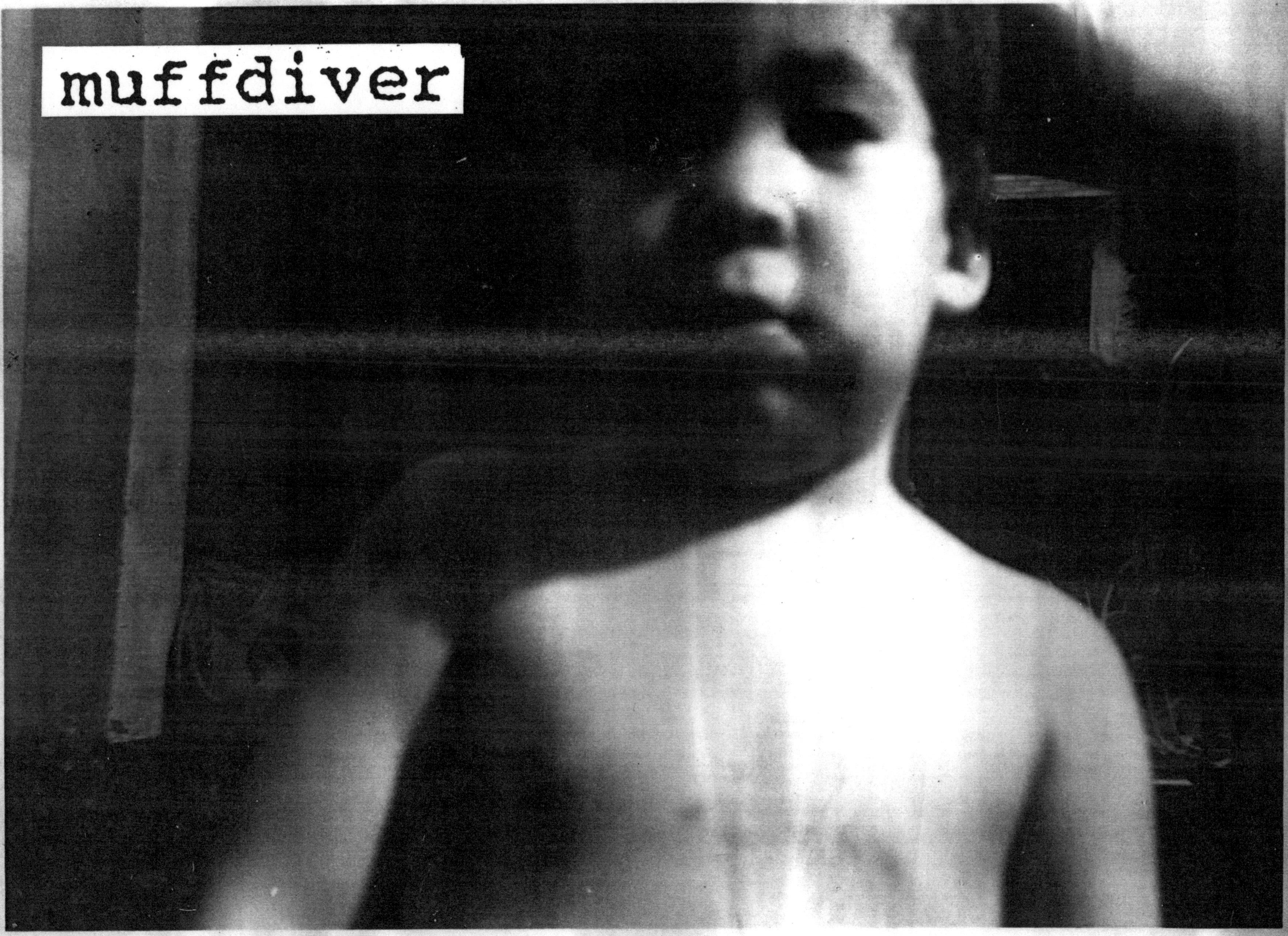

muffdiver

fierce pussy

find

the

dyke

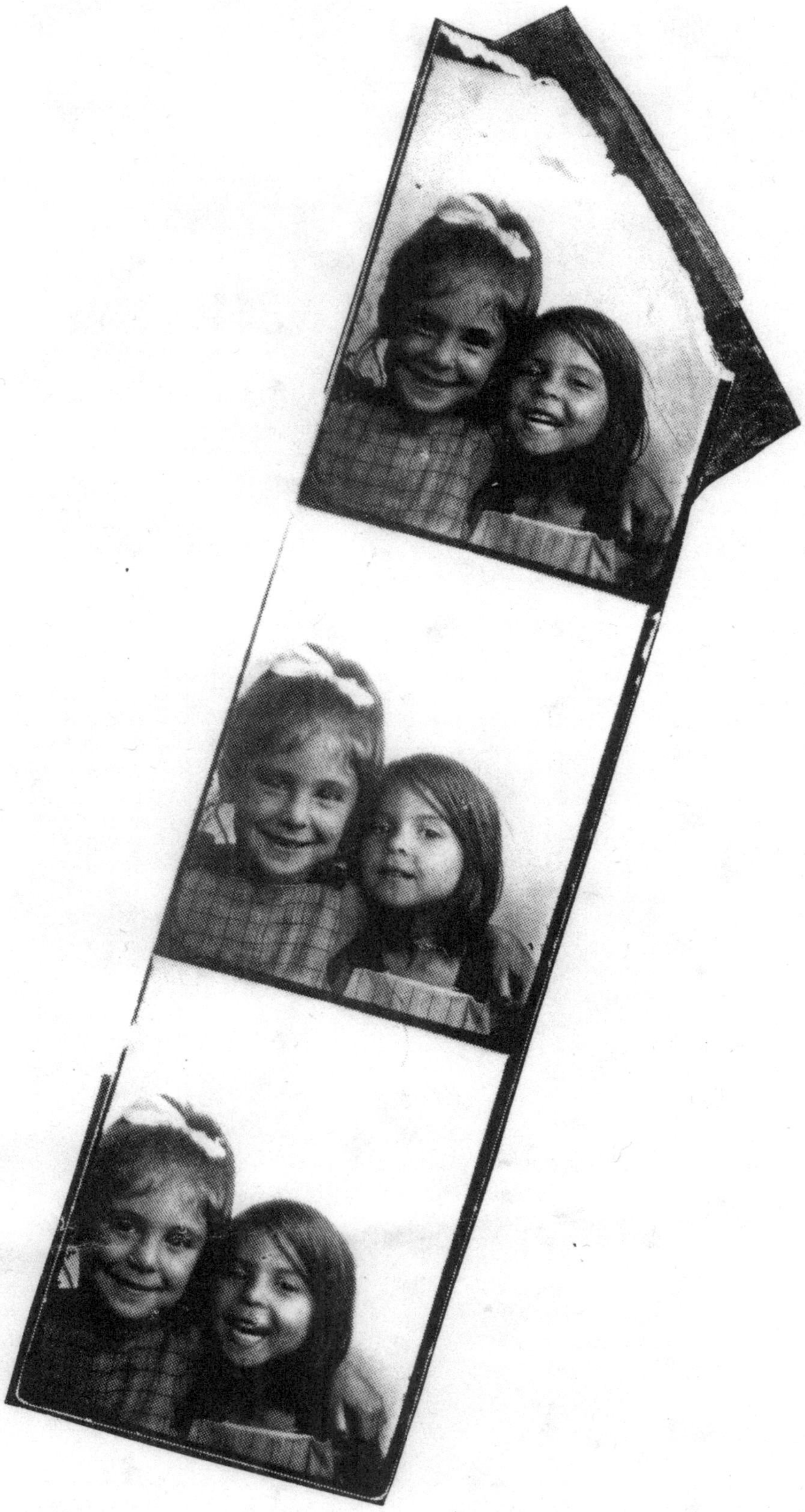

in this

picture.

fierce pussy

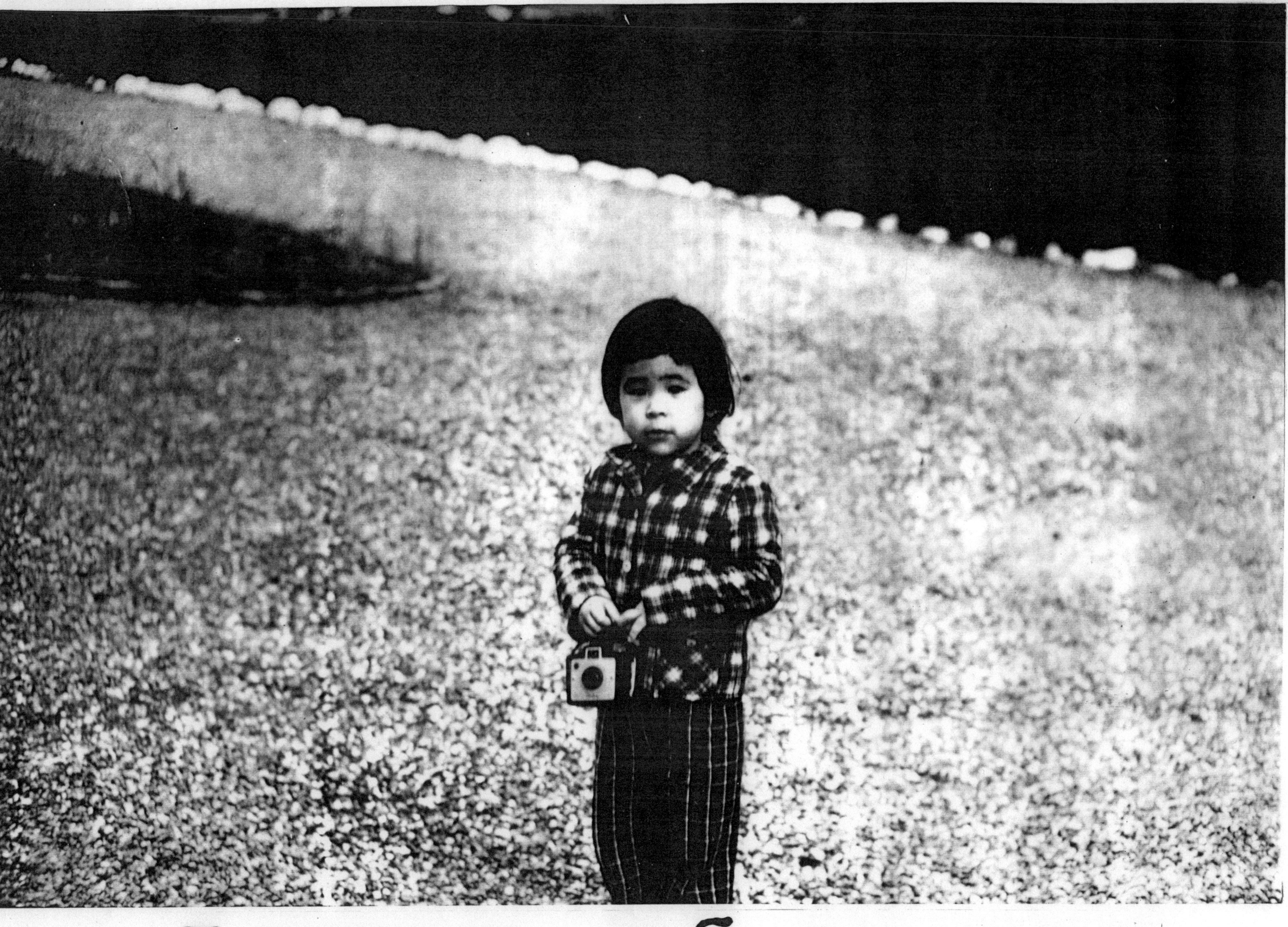

Lover of women

fierce pussy

JUL • 59 •

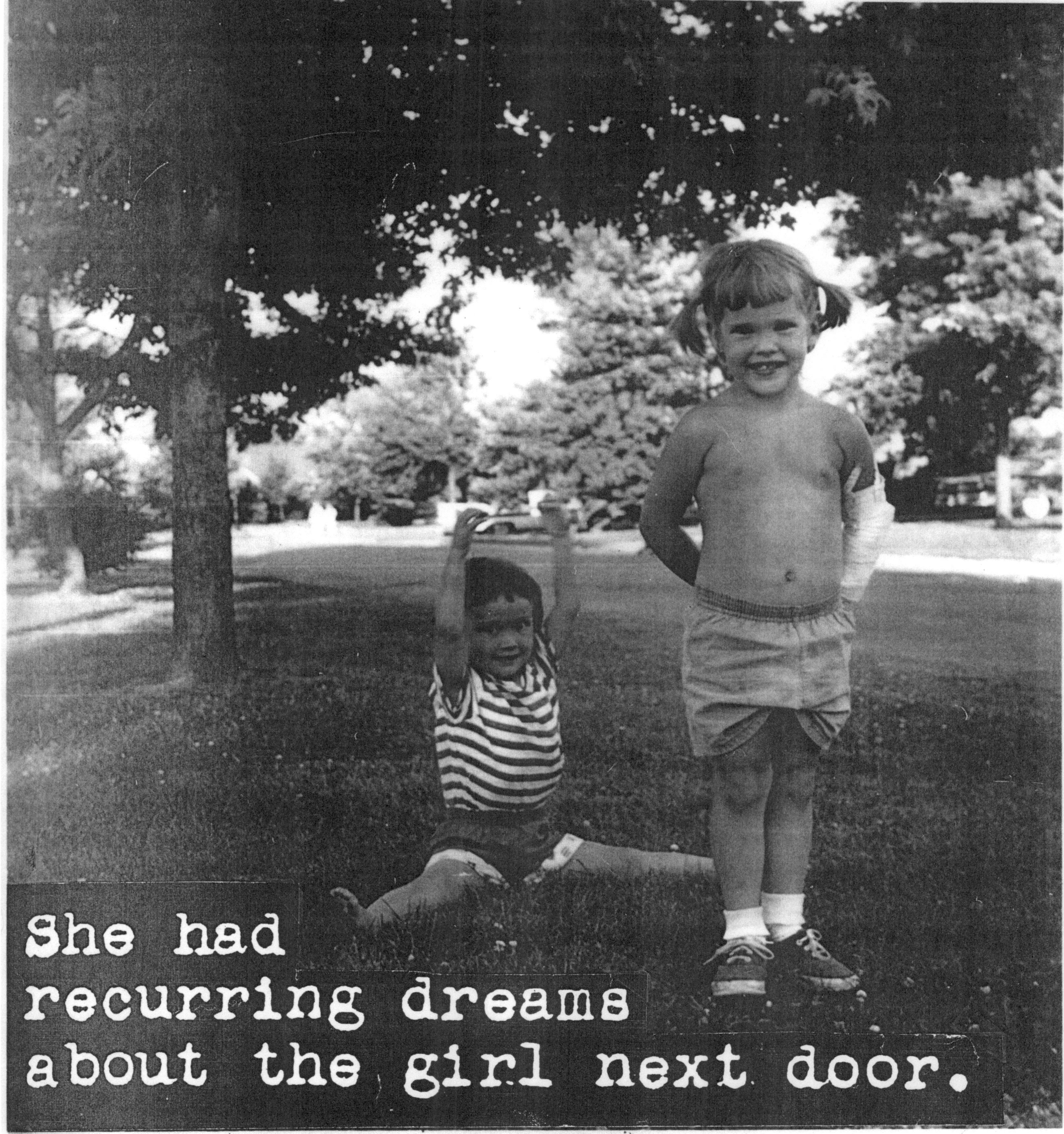

fierce pussy

Are you a

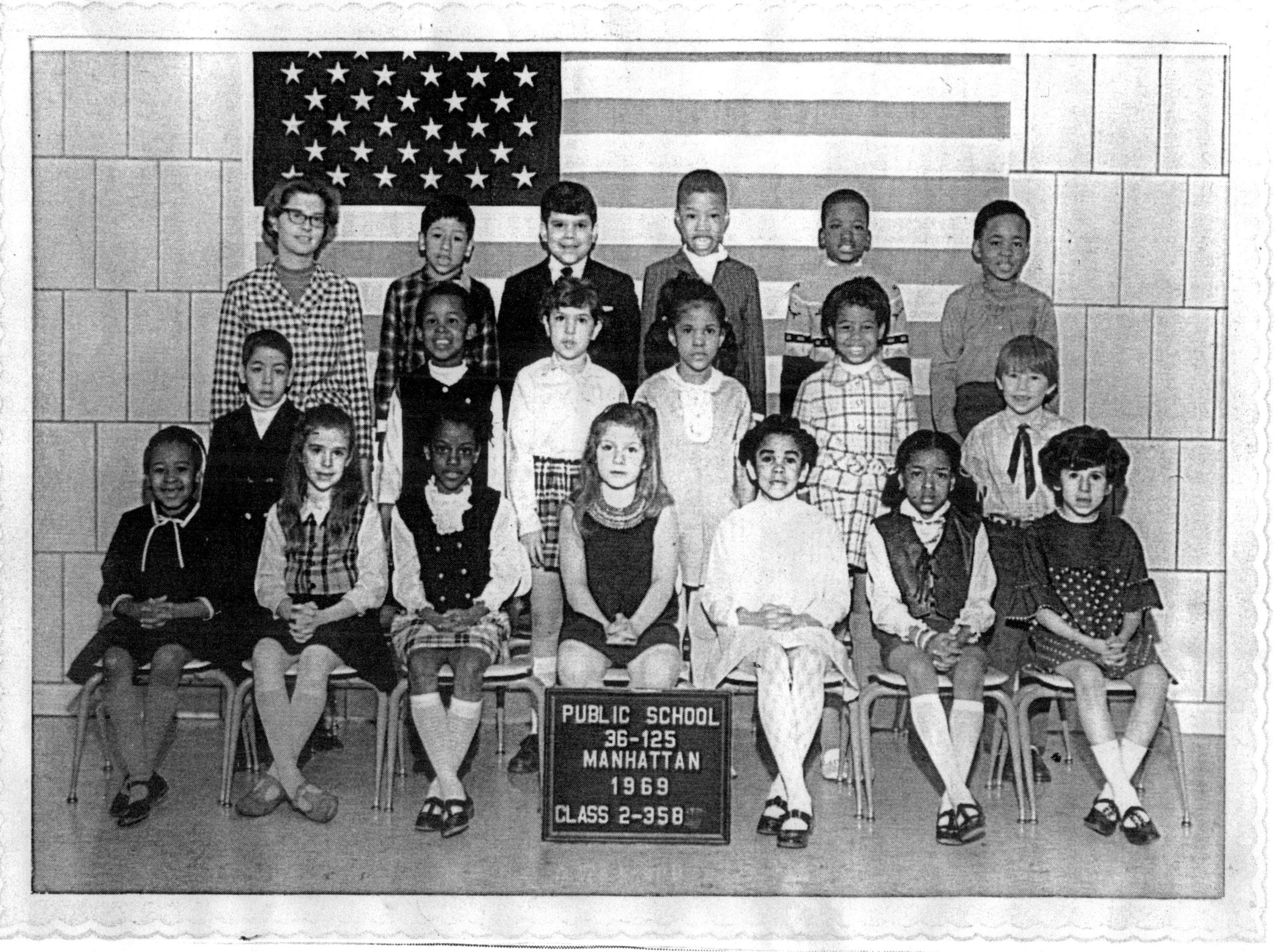

boy or a girl?

fierce pussy

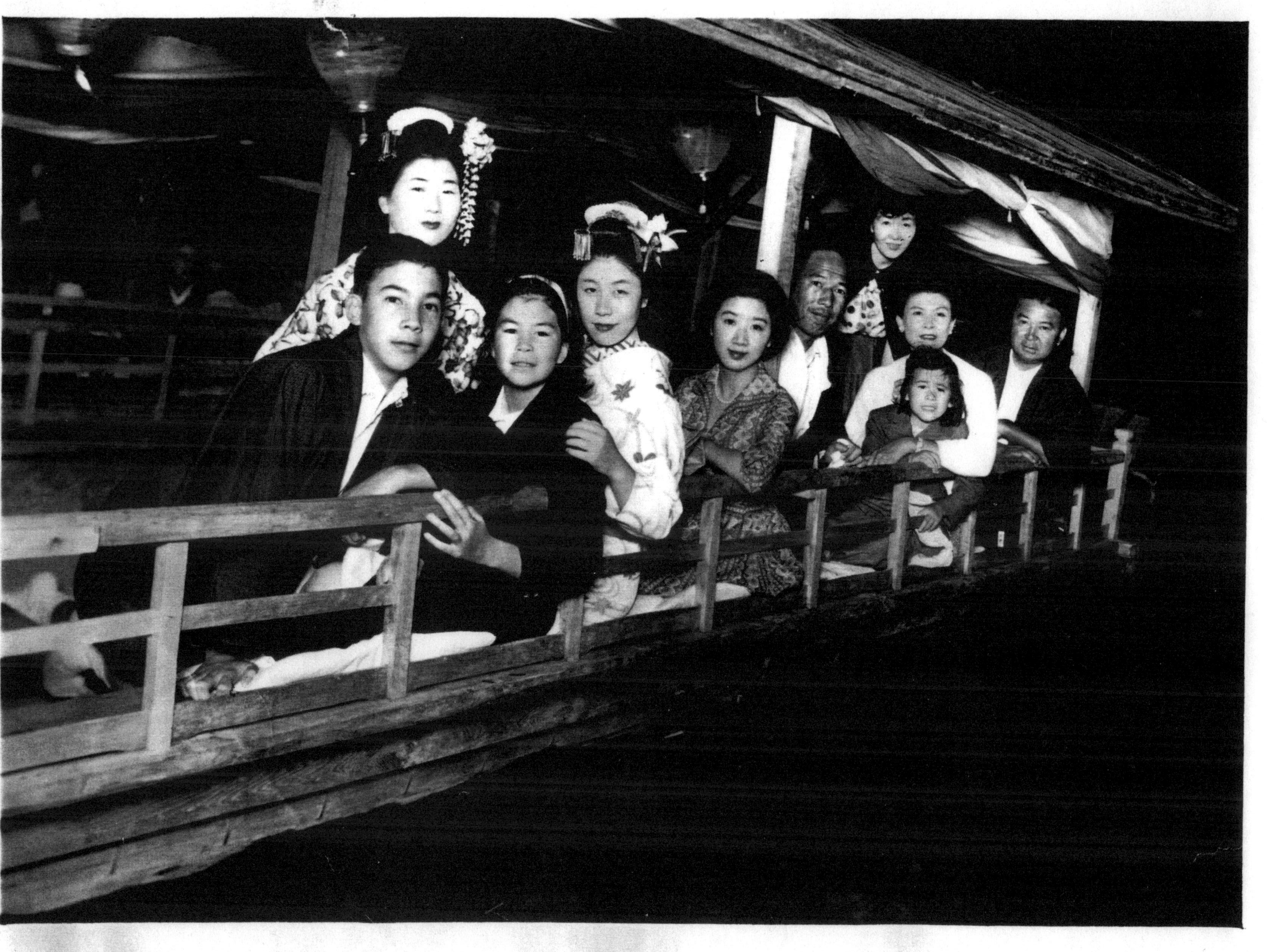

find the dyke in this picture

fierce pussy

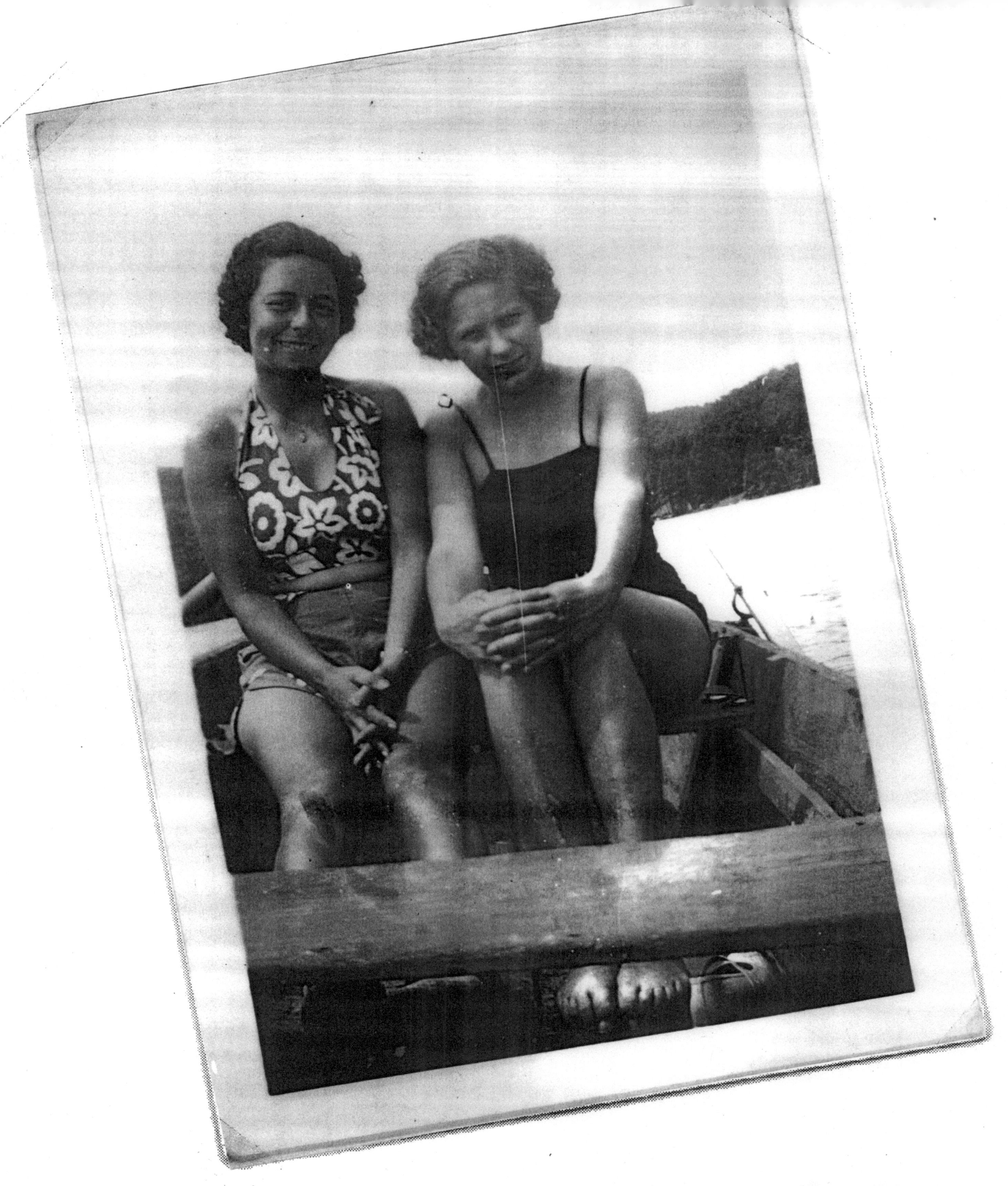

we just really enjoy each other

fierce pussy

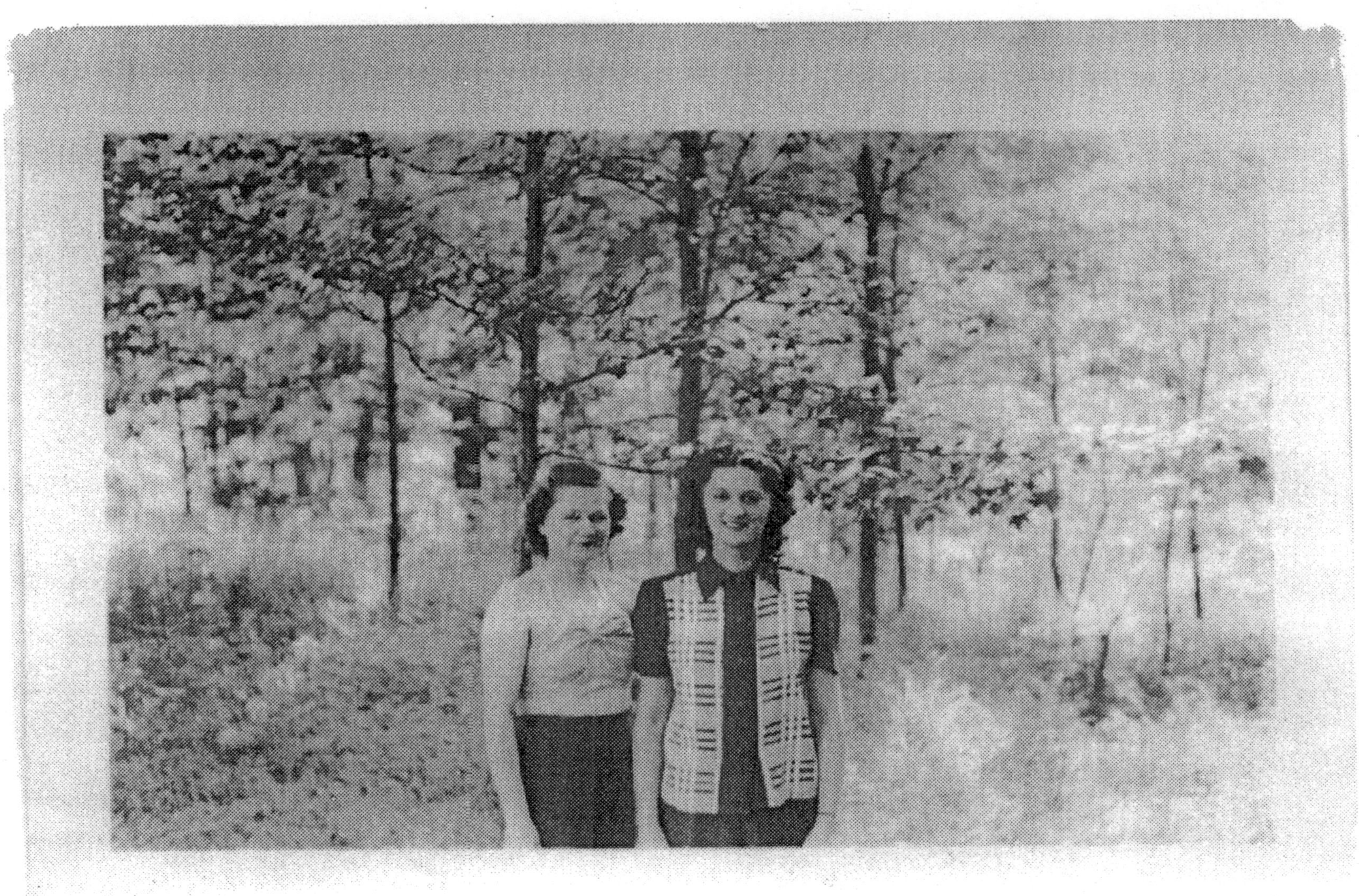

companions?

fierce pussy

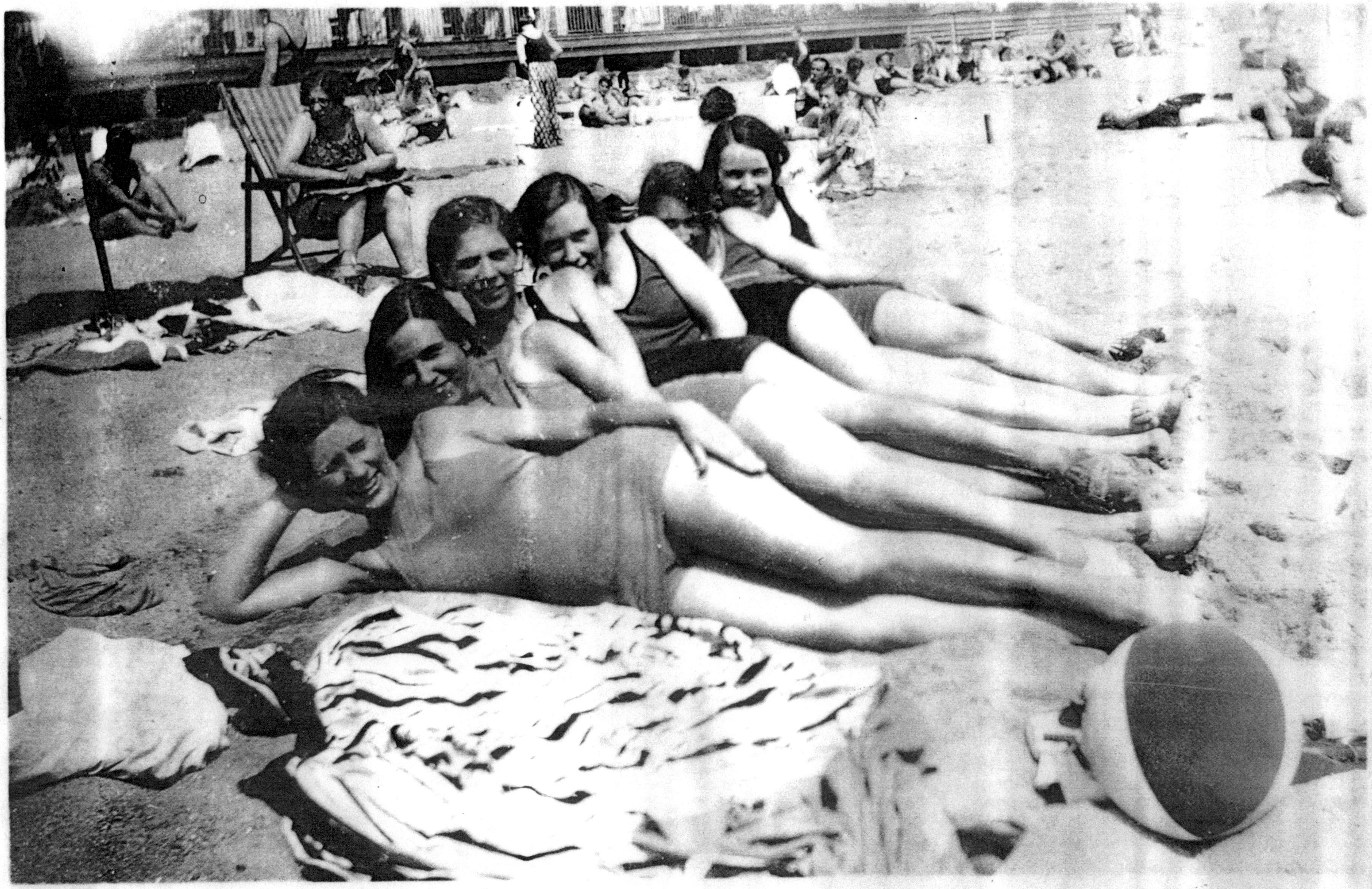

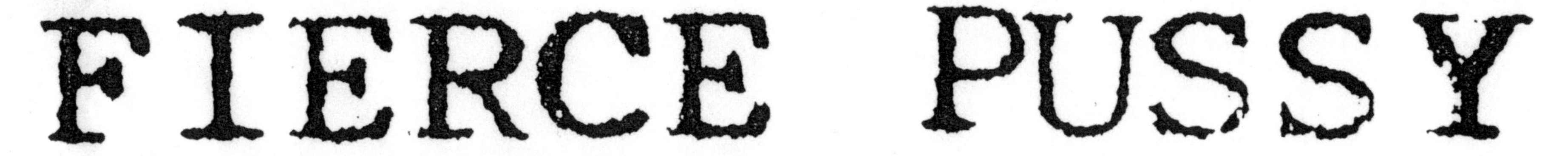
FIERCE PUSSY

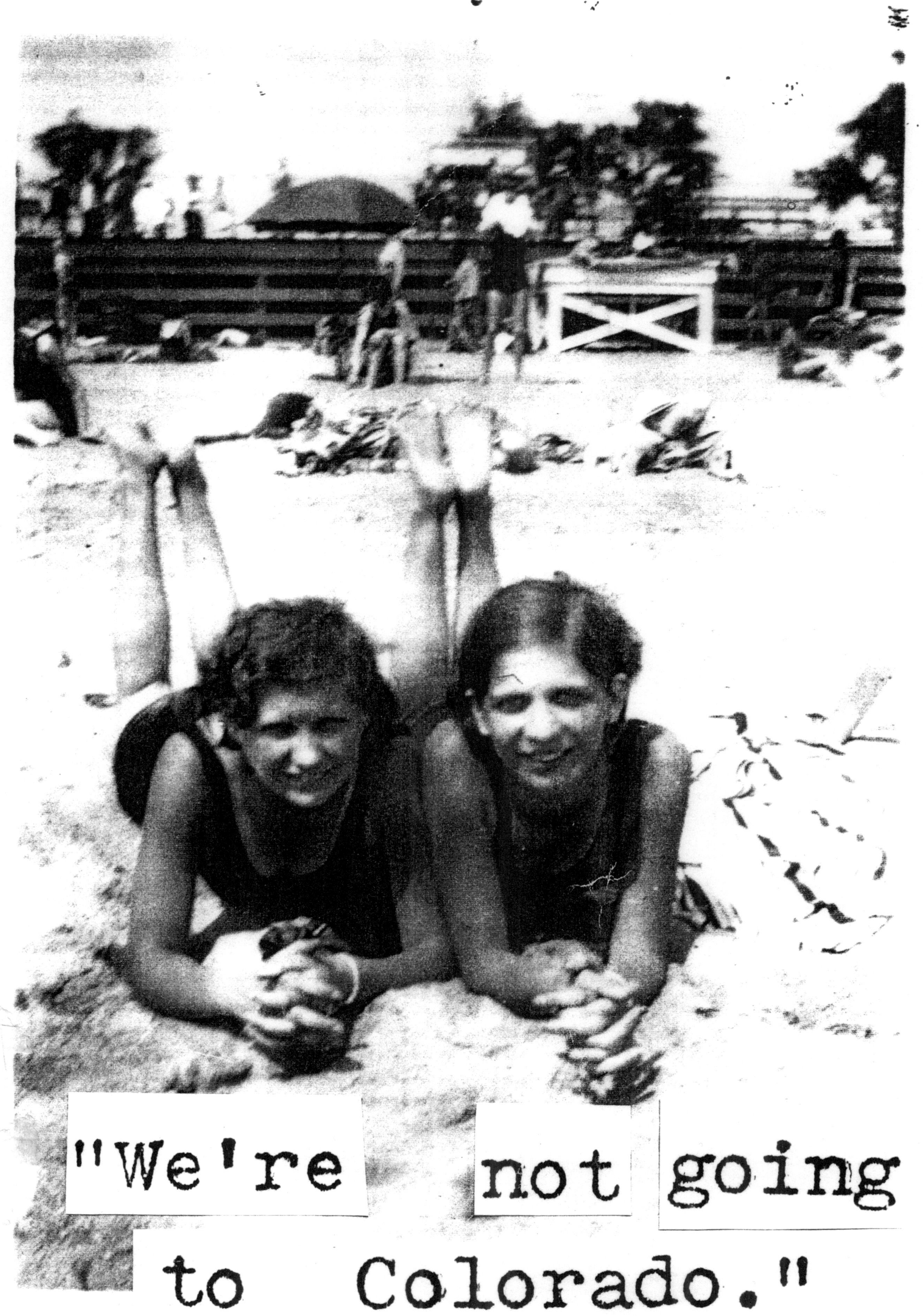

fierce pussy

what is a lesbian?

your veterinarian
your nurse
your favorite movie star
your lawyer
your teacher
your gynecologist
your dentist
your sanitation worker
your butcher
your boss
your sister
your sergeant
your psychiatrist
your waitress
your cop
your receptionist
your girlfriend

fierce pussy

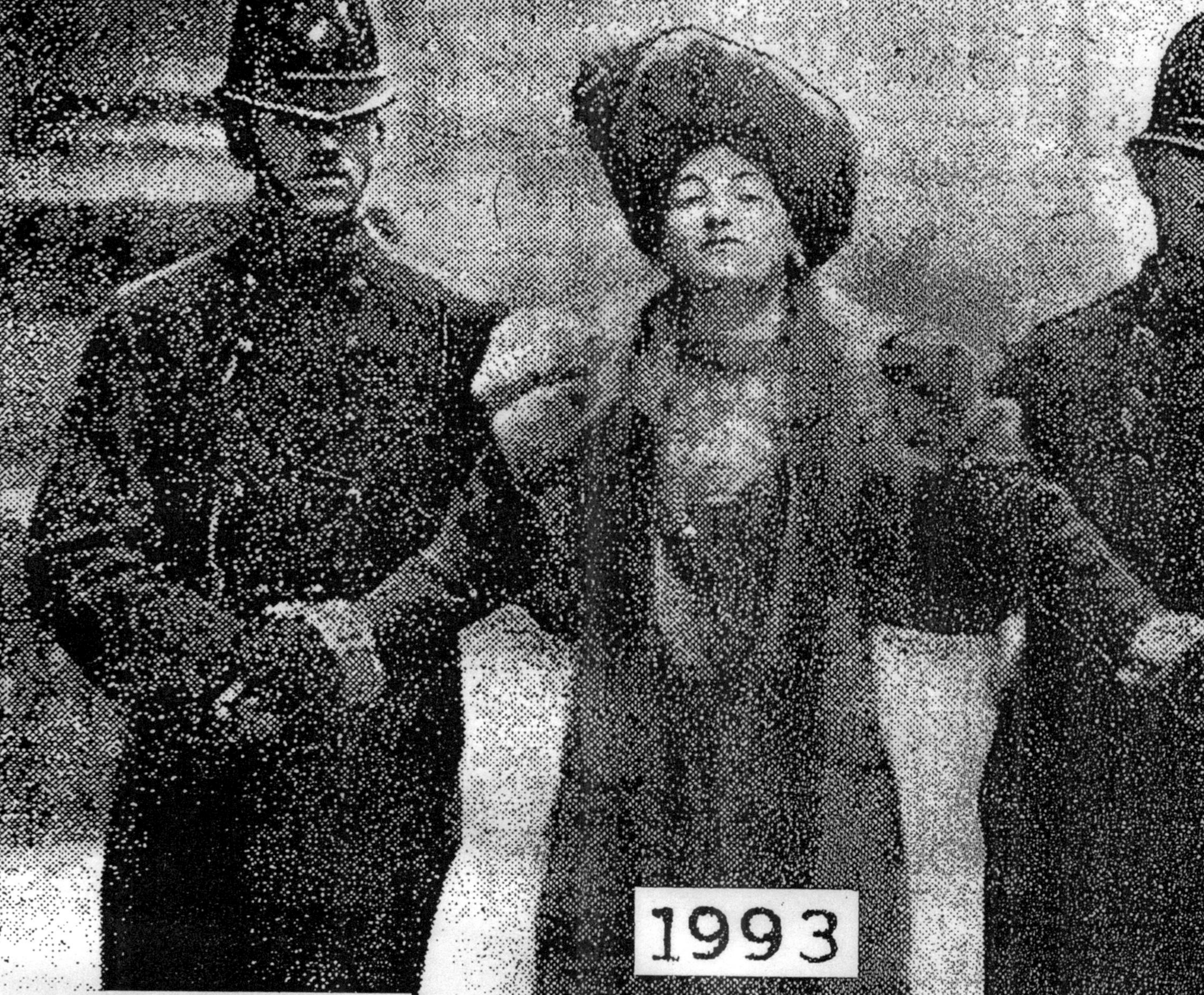

fierce pussy

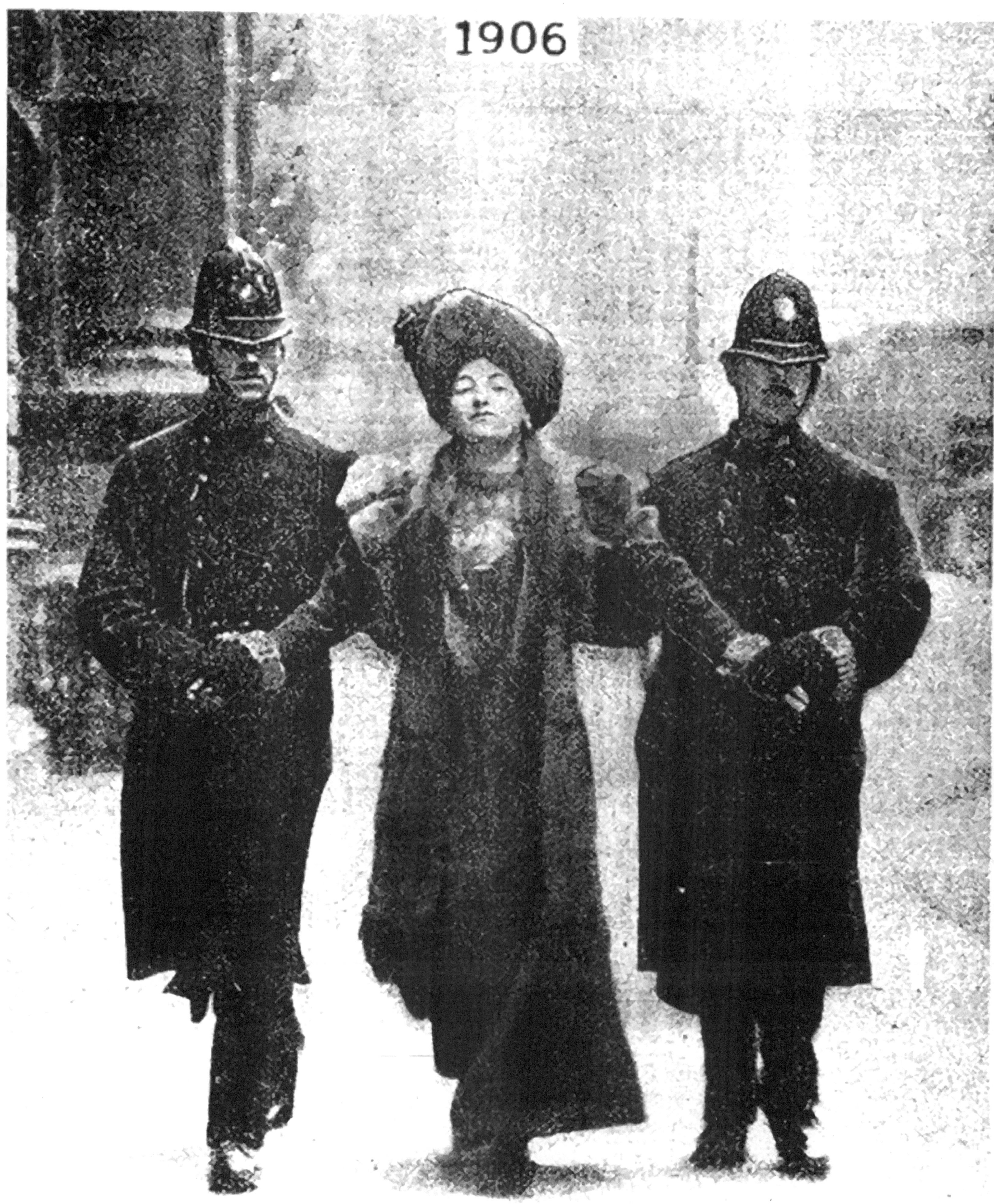

fierce pussy

LESBIAN CHIC

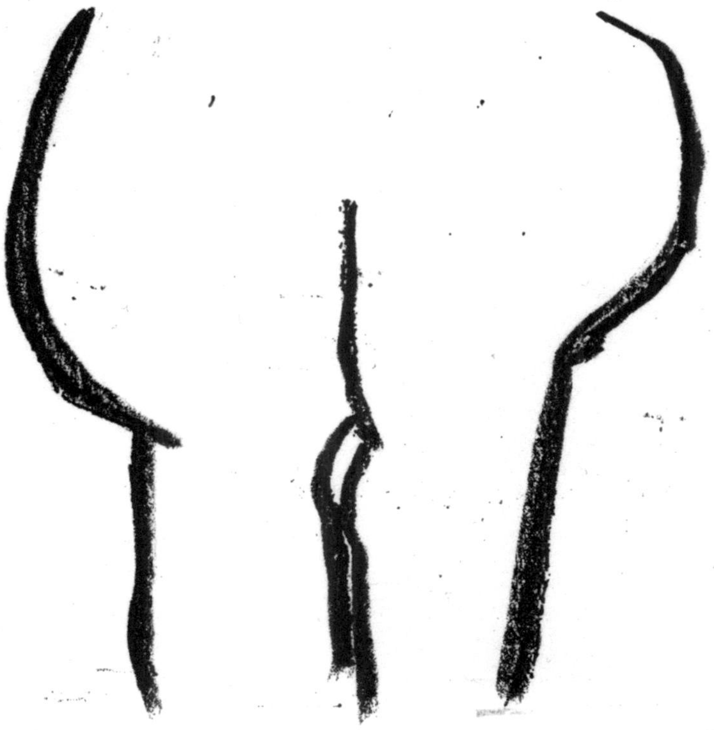

MY ASS

Fuck 15 minutes of fame.

We demand our civil rights.

Now.

fierce pussy

MANASSAS, Va. — A 26-year-old suburban Washington man whose wife cut off his penis with a kitchen knife while he slept was reported in satisfactory condition after 9½ hours of surgery to reattach the organ, officials said.

Authorities learned of the incident when the man showed up at a local hospital about 5 a.m. Police officers were dispatched to search for the missing penis, but couldn't find it.

About the same time, the man's wife called authorities to say she had been raped, had fled "in a panic," unknowingly taking the penis with her, and had thrown the penis out the window of her car near the city line

The penis was recovered, packed in ice and taken by fire and rescue personnel to Prince William Hospital, where the surgical reattachment took place.

The woman told police that her husband had raped her shortly before she cut off two-thirds of his penis.

Next time we'll bury it.

fierce pussy

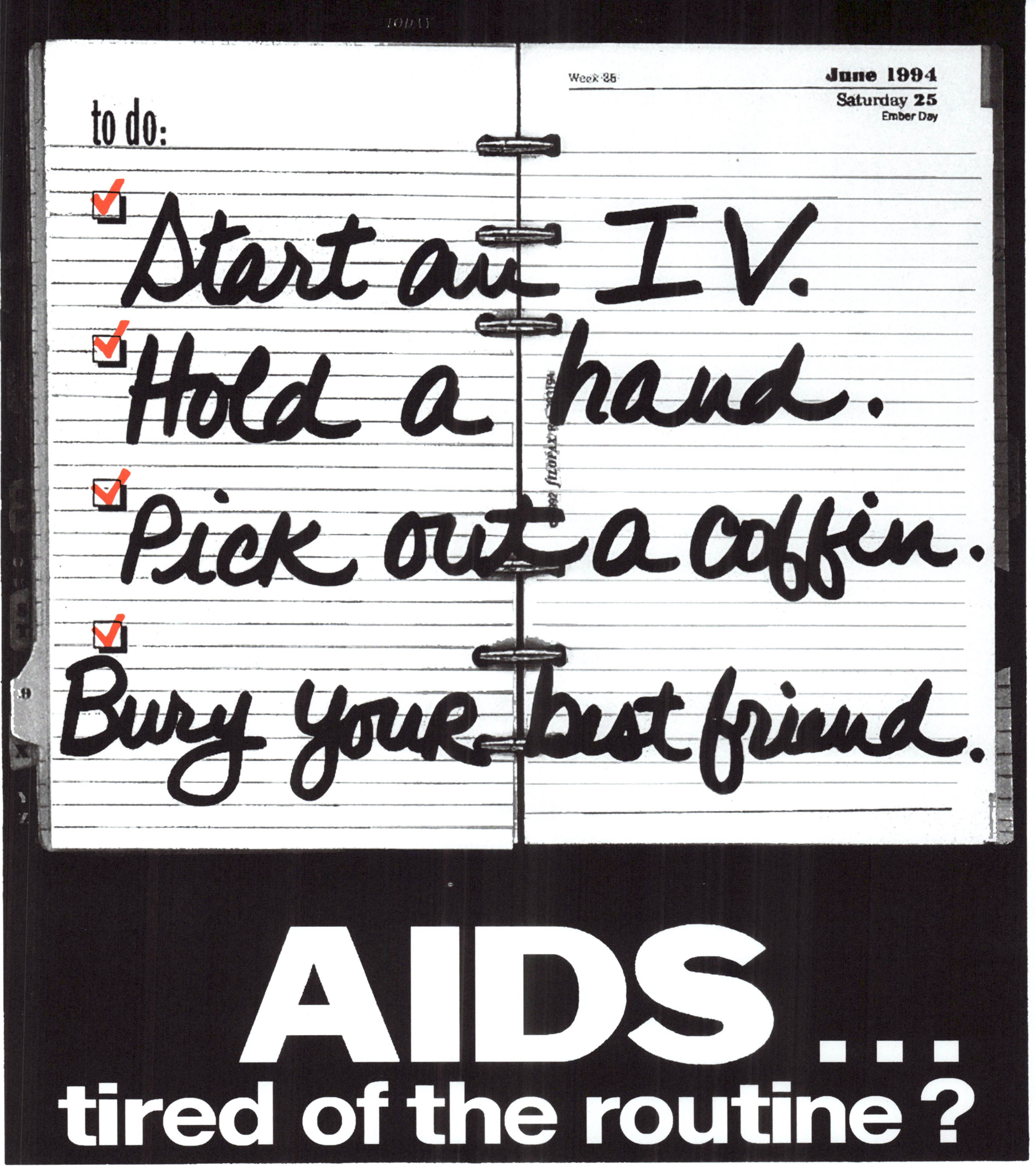

Be enraged.

Become explosive.

fierce pussy

I AM A
lezzie
butch
pervert
feminist
amazon
bulldagger
dyke
AND SO ARE YOU

dresses or skirts. Her case history is both interesting and typical. But it is decidedly not pleasant.

James and Margaret Taft had two other children before they had Bobby. Both were boys, and neither lived more than four months. The first was born prematurely and died almost at once. The second, born a year later, was a healthy baby who managed to pick up a virus that was strong enough to prove fatal.

When Bobby was born two years later, the Tafts were a little disappointed. They had wanted a boy all along, and the two boys who had not lived only piled fuel on the fire. Bobby's room in their flat on Chicago's South Side was painted a bright baby blue. Bobby's clothes were primarily the boy's clothing that her two brothers never got a chance to wear. These were small factors, but they established a pattern in the Taft family which in itself helped to mold and shape Bobby's psychological development.

While neither James nor Marge Taft realized it, Bobby was a son who happened to be a girl. The stories her father read to her were adventure stories. For presents she received a baseball glove, athletic equipment, toys designed for boys, not for girls. On summer evenings she played catch with her father in the back yard.

Today those games of catch remain the strongest memories of her early childhood. "Mom would be in the kitchen, making dinner or doing the dishes," she says. "And Dad and I would be out in back tossing a ball back and forth. In the fall it was a football, in the spring and summer a baseball. Mom would do the housework and I would play catch with Dad."

The psychological inference here is obvious. Bobby automatically identified herself with her father, and thus with men in general. Her mother was doing housework, woman's work, while she and her father played

a masculine game. A clear d
manner. Cooking and dishwasl
and football for boys. Bobby w
the fence.

Bobby was naturally athle
encouragement which she rece
her athletic development. She v
In school and after school, she
to play with the boys.

She could run as fast, thro
a baseball bat as effectively as
she didn't cry when she got
taught at home that crying w
accepted her as a playmate al
When they went through the ty
where association with girls w
Bobby was an exception to the
boys," and they didn't mind hav

It might be wise to pause here
point that a great number of gi
stage similar to Bobby's with n
The overwhelming majority of
out of this stage and into high
with no trouble at all. They
children, and lead lives as normal
as any other women do. But in B
role was too much a function of
development to be so easily ca
of adolescence.

A significant change in the
Bobby's first year in high school
suddenly turned into young wor
their shyness and dated them.

Bobby did not get many dates
she was not a pretty girl as beca
boys, she was still "one of the f

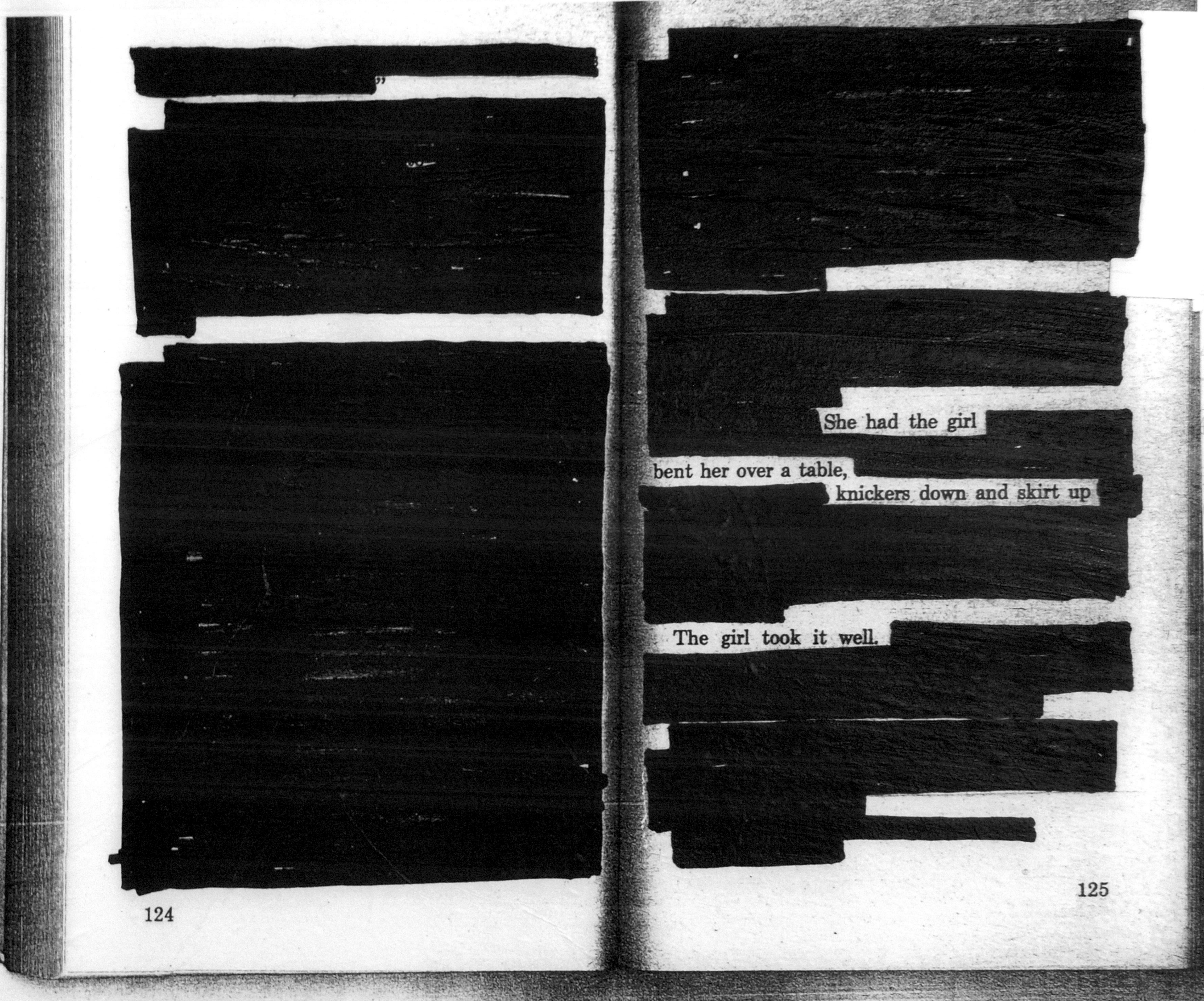

fierce pussy

ten strokes

mistress

thumping whip

pony dance

her bottom

wooden trestle.

cheeks apart,

spread.

wander the alleys, frequent the bars, take on lover after lover

if he were alive today he’d be standing next to you if she were alive today you’d be texting her right now if he were alive today he’d be going gray if they were alive today I wonder what pronoun they’d be using if he were alive today he’d still be living with AIDS if he were alive today he would be at this opening if she were alive today she could tell you about getting arrested at City Hall if he were alive today you would have met him by now if she were alive today you’d be just her type if he were alive today he’d be outside smoking if they were alive today they’d still be living with AIDS if she were alive today she’d be having a hot flash they were alive today they would have finished writing that book if he were alive today he have you on your knees if they were alive today you’d still be sharing an office if she were alive today she’d laugh at that if he were alive today I wonder if they would have gotten married she were alive today she’d be going down on you tonight if he were alive today you could ask him about that if she were alive today she still couldn’t afford healthcare if they were alive today you’d have such a crush on them if she were alive today she’d be out walking the dog if he were alive today you’d probably still be arguing about that if she were alive today maybe she’d have a gallery by now if he were alive today he’d never let them get away with that if he were alive today we’d be going dancing later if she were alive today she’d tie you up and spank you if he were alive today do you think he would have gotten sober if they were alive today they’d know exactly what to say if she were alive today she’d still be living with AIDS if he were alive today he’d have his arm around you if he were alive today he’d be in this picture

fierce pussy *For The Record* 2016

tomgirl

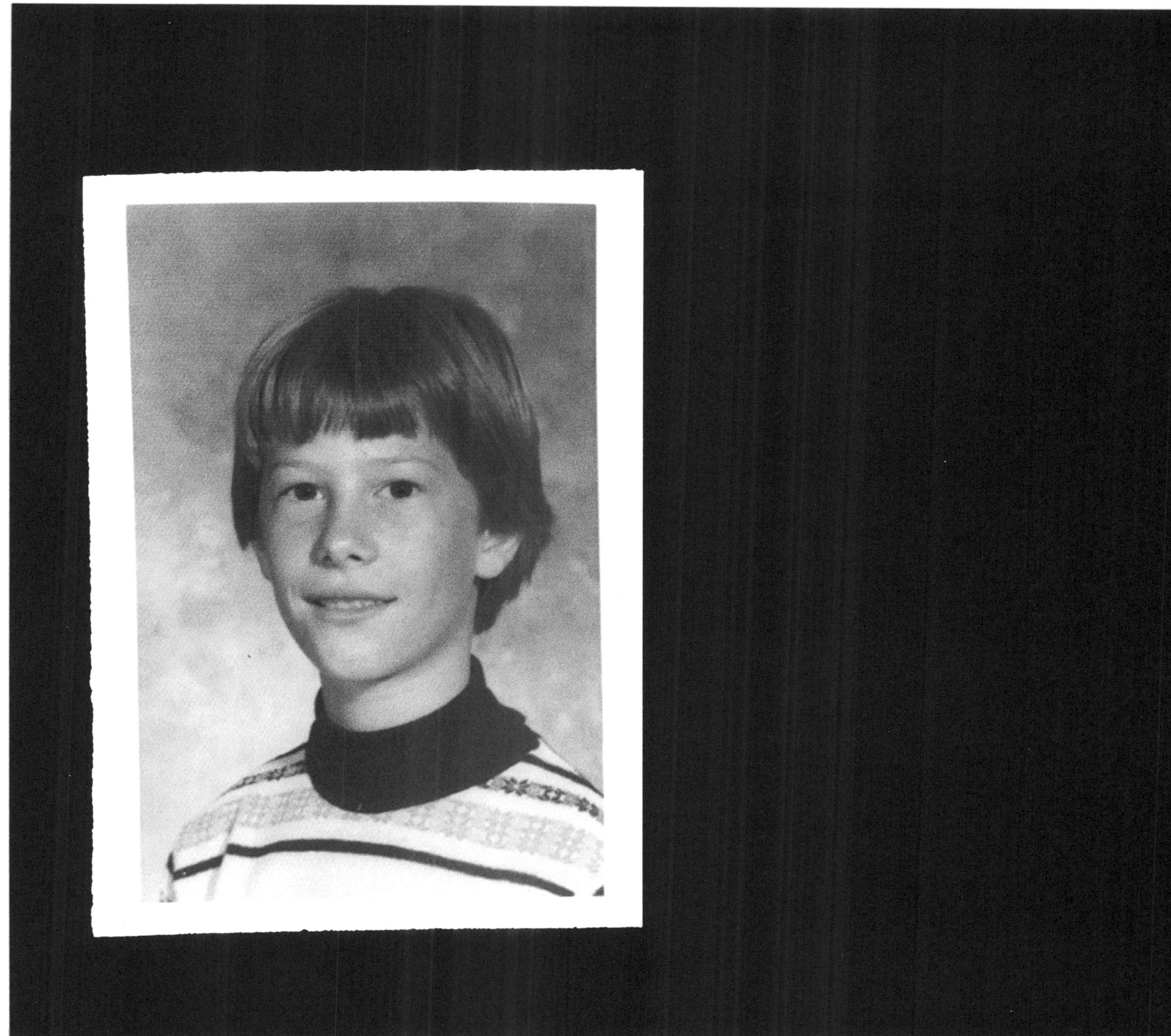

fierce pussy

bulldagger

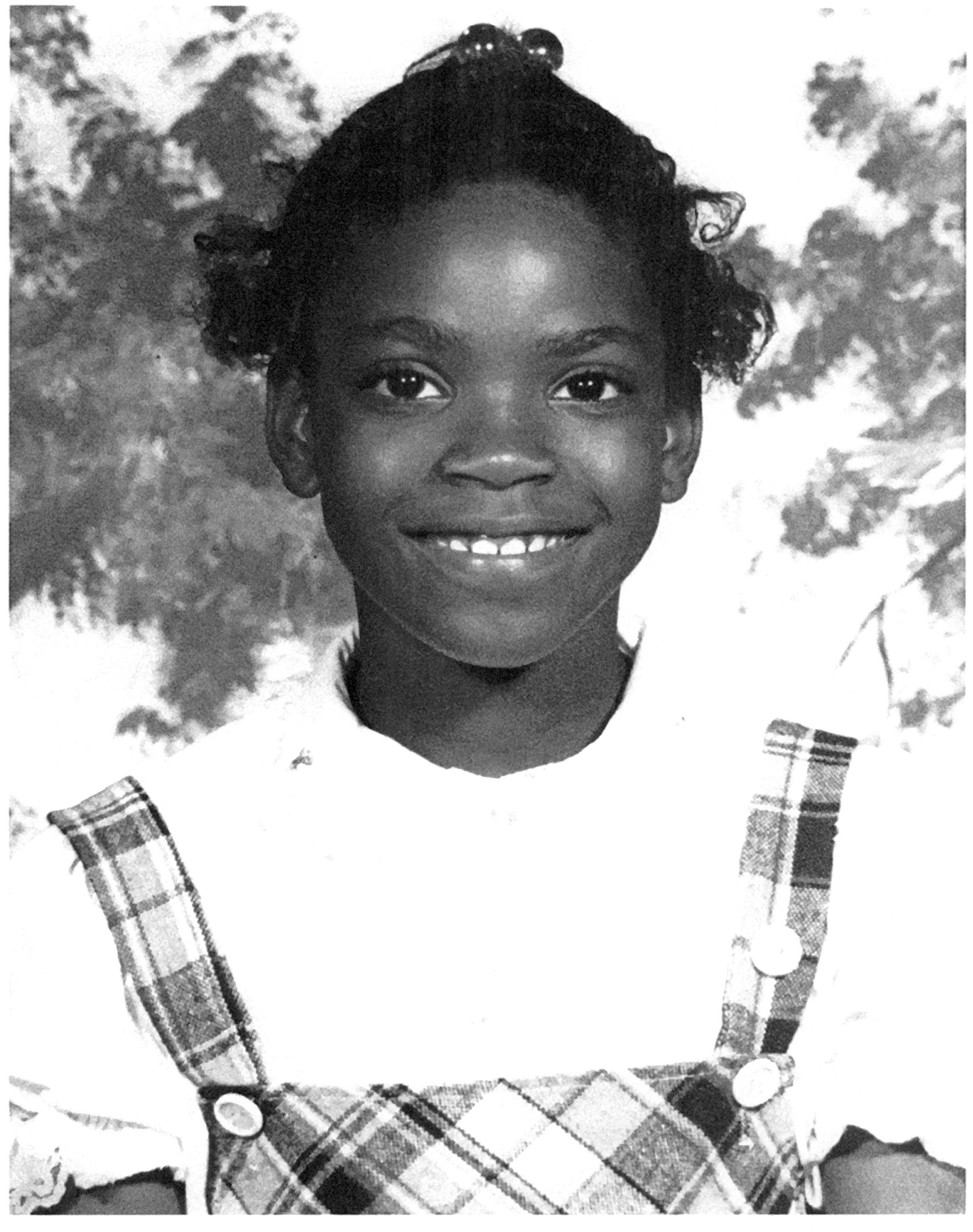

fierce pussy

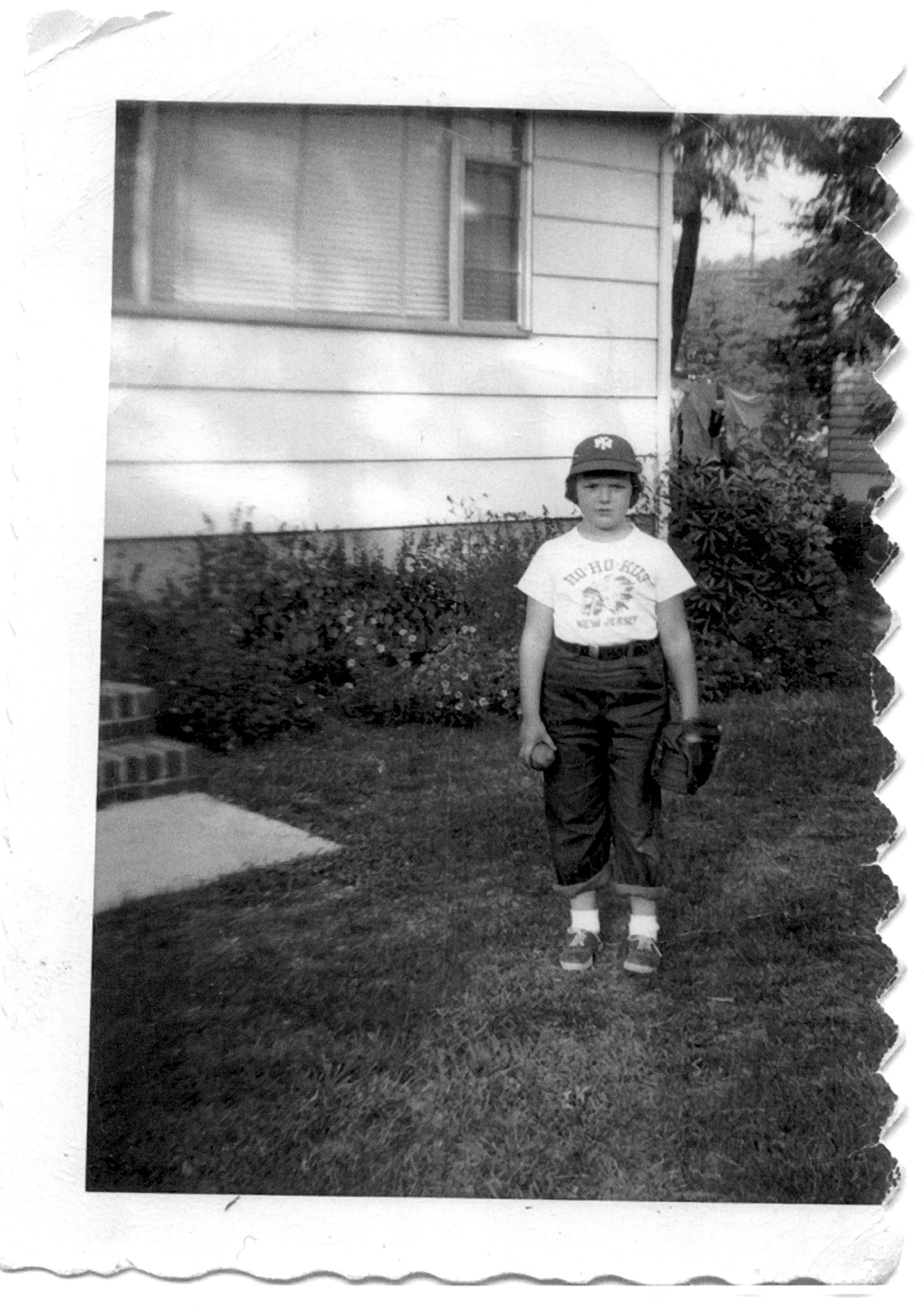

fierce pussy

I AM A
queer
androgyme
feminist
trannie
pervert
stone butch
tomgirl
dyke
AND SO ARE YOU

fierce pussy

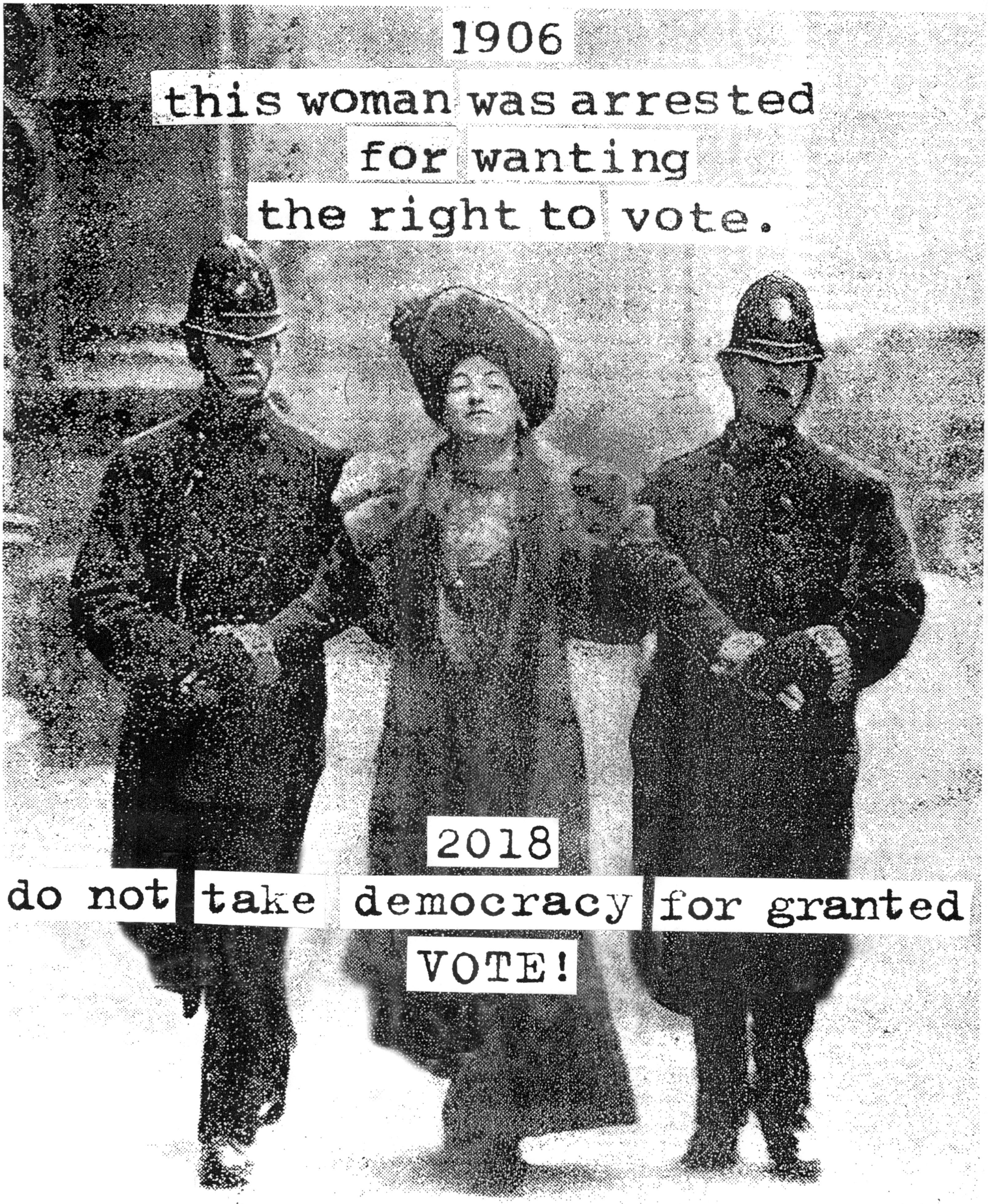

1906

this woman was arrested
for wanting
the right to vote.

2018

do not take democracy for granted

VOTE!

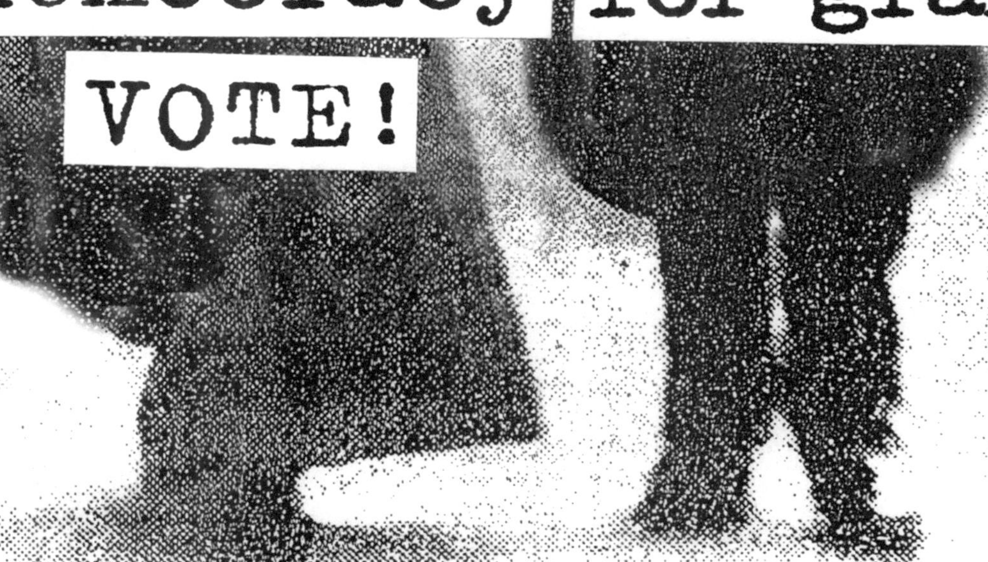

fierce pussy

I AM A
queer
bulldagger
fairy
feminist
butch
pervert
trannie
muffdiver
homo
tomgirl
dyke
AND SO ARE YOU

fierce pussy

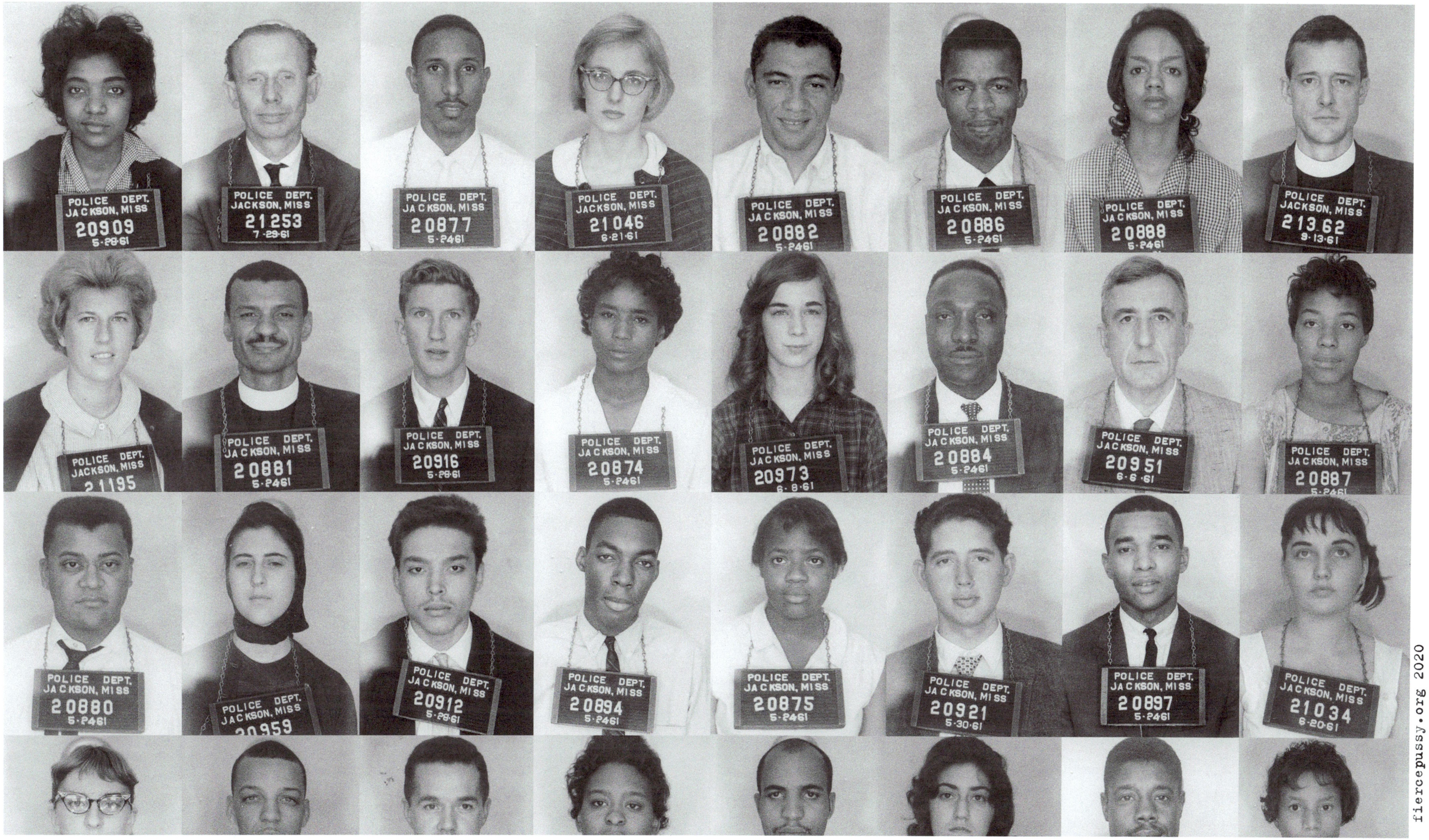

fiercepussy.org 2020

Freedom Riders Jackson Mississippi 1961

PEOPLE HAVE THE POWER
WE HAVE THE POWER. VOTE

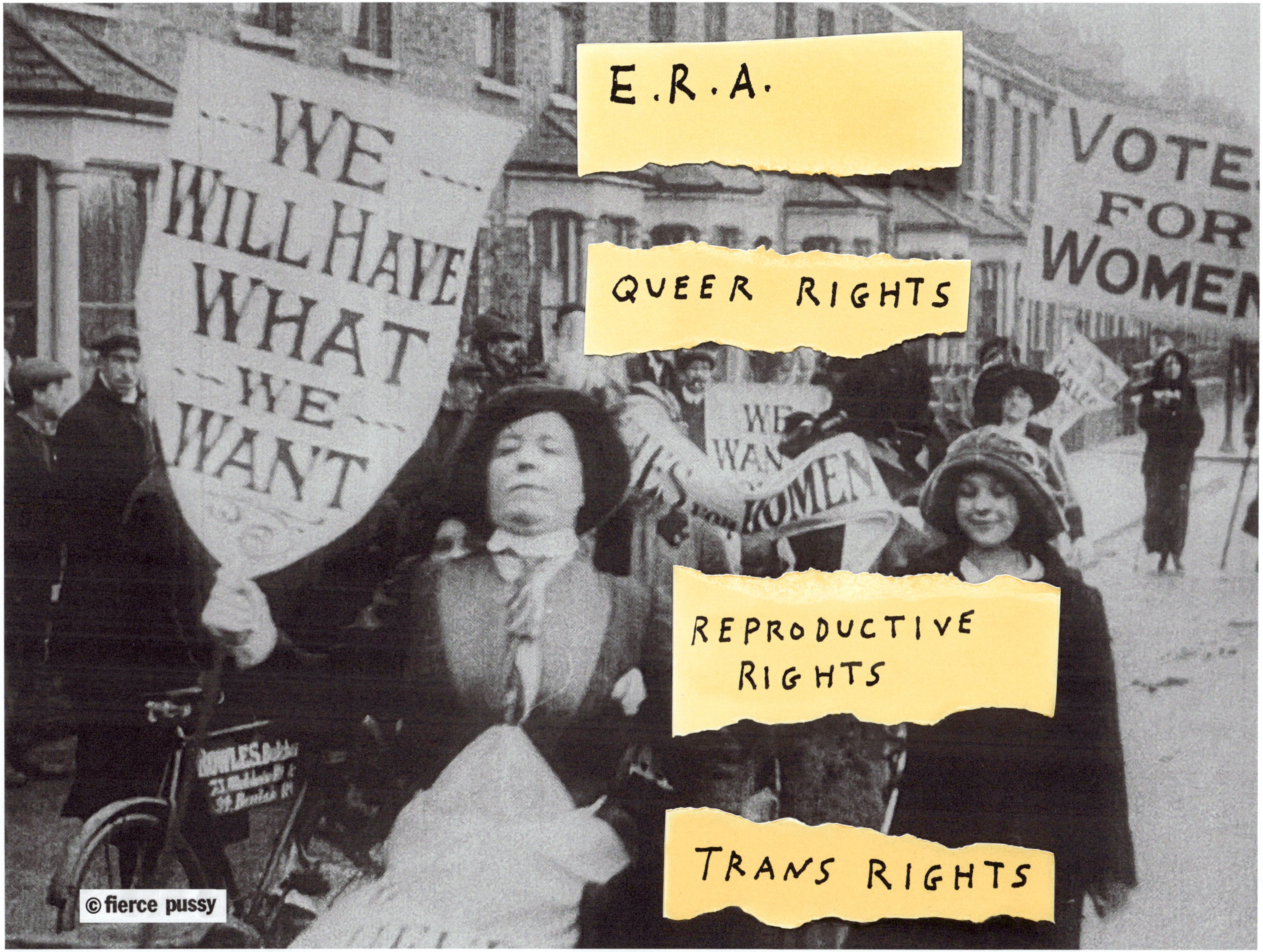

WE WILL HAVE WHAT WE WANT

E.R.A.

QUEER RIGHTS

VOTE FOR WOMEN

REPRODUCTIVE RIGHTS

TRANS RIGHTS

ich bin ein*e

lesbe

queer

früchtchen

kampflesbe

tunte

böse möse

butch

transe

schwuchtel

mannsweib

emanze

so wie du auch!

fierce pussy

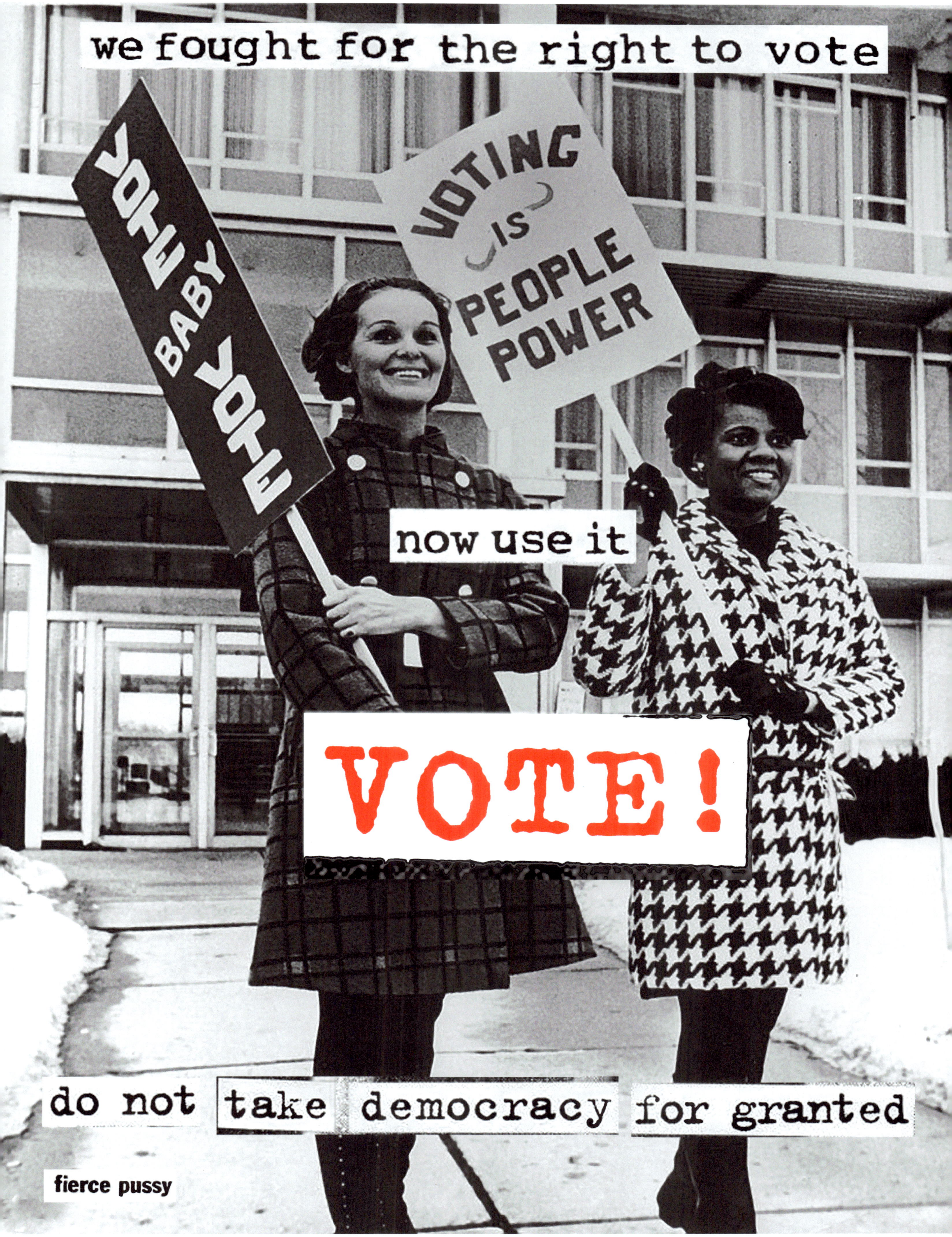

we fought for the right to vote

now use it

VOTE!

do not take democracy for granted

fierce pussy

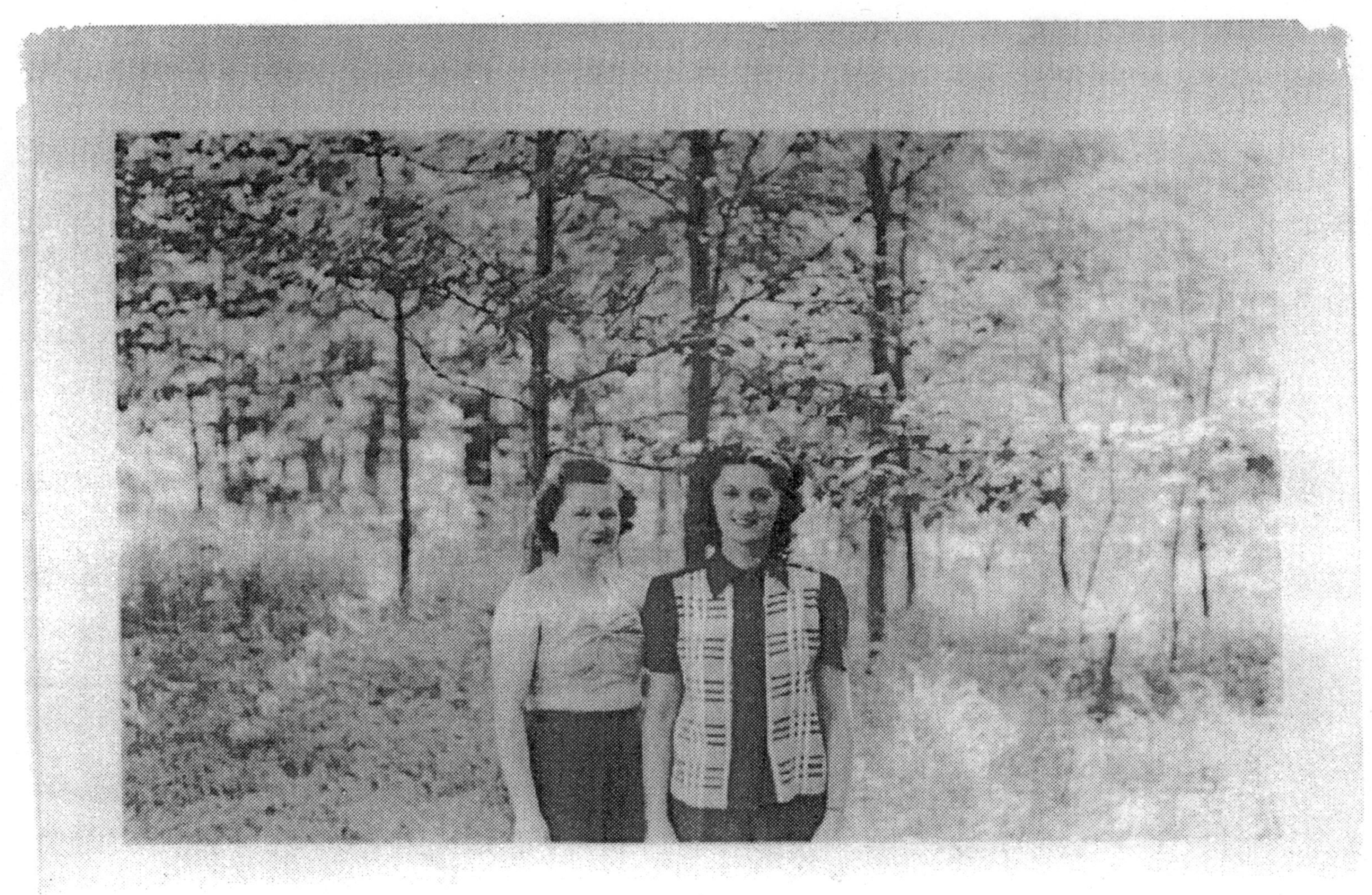

companheiras?

fierce pussy

I

got

all

my

sisters

with

me

fierce pussy 2025

“we are family” written by bernard edwards & nile rodgers, recorded by sister sledge in 1979

fierce pussy is an art collective formed in 1991 in New York City by a group of Queer women committed to creating public art and performing direct action around issues of lesbian and LGBTQ+ identity, visibility, and rights.

Early fierce pussy projects included: wheatpasting posters on the street, renaming New York City streets after prominent lesbian heroines, redesigning the restroom at The Lesbian, Gay, Bisexual & Transgender Community Center, creating a greeting card campaign directed at Cardinal John O'Connor and Senator Alfonse D'Amato, printing and distributing stickers and t-shirts, and making our own moving billboard/truck.

From 1991 to 1994, fierce pussy was composed of a fluid and often-shifting cadre of dykes. Core members were Pam Brandt, Nancy Brooks Brody, Joy Episalla, Alison Froling, Zoe Leonard, Suzanne Wright, and Carrie Yamaoka. Many others attended an occasional meeting, or came out to wheatpaste, stencil, sticker, or drive the truck around the city.

Adamantly fast, lo-tech, and low-budget, we relied on our own modest resources. We used our old typewriters, our own baby pictures, and whatever material we could get donated. We used equipment at our day jobs to produce the work. Emerging during a decade steeped in the urgency of the AIDS crisis and LGBTQ+ activism, fierce pussy brought Queer identity directly into the streets. In recent years we have expanded to also present our work in galleries and museums, while continuing to intervene in public space, always working with an economy of means and a collective ethos of inclusion and solidarity.

The first edition of this book was published in conjunction with the collective's 2008 exhibition at Printed Matter. At that time, the four core founding members Nancy Brooks Brody (1962–2023), Joy Episalla, Zoe Leonard, and Carrie Yamaoka began working together again. The Printed Matter edition included sixteen fierce pussy posters in an oversized format with spiral binding.

This expanded edition published by Primary Information retains the original flexible design and includes several earlier posters not in the first edition as well as a number of more recent posters.

Feel free to share, post, copy, distribute, wheatpaste, and circulate these posters.

http://www.fiercepussy.org

Poster Chronology

1991 *I AM A lezzie . . . AND PROUD!*
I AM A stone butch . . . AND PROUD
I AM A mannish . . . AND PROUD!
Dyke
lesbian
muffdiver
find the dyke in this picture.
Lover of women
She had recurring dreams about the girl next door.
Are you a boy or a girl?
find the dyke in this picture
we just really enjoy each other
companions?
FIERCE PUSSY

1992 *"We're not going to Colorado."* : This poster was conceived in solidarity with the Boycott Colorado campaign, in response to the passage of anti-LGBTQ+ state legislation.

1993 *what is a lesbian?*
Suffragette 1993
Suffragette 1906
LESBIAN CHIC
Next time we'll bury it.

1994 *AIDS . . . tired of the routine?* : This poster was originally produced as a moving billboard for the fierce pussy truck that circulated around New York during Pride weekend.

2008 *AND SO ARE YOU* : This poster was made for the retrospective *fierce pussy*, held at Printed Matter, New York, curated by AA Bronson.

2009 *Bobby*
The girl took it well.
pony dance
wander the alleys
These four posters were part of *gutter*, a series developed during fierce pussy's residency at the Lesbian Herstory Archives, New York.

2017 *For the Record* : This text was originally written by fierce pussy as part of the project *Get Up Everybody and Sing*, 2010, and was reconceived for the endpapers of Élisabeth Lebovici's book *Ce que le sida m'a fait*, JRP Editions, 2017.

2018 *tomgirl* : This poster was made in collaboration with Justin Vivian Bond.
bulldagger : This poster was made in collaboration with Heather Lynn Johnson.
fierce pussy : This poster was made in collaboration with Barbara Hughes.
AND SO ARE YOU
These four posters were made for *fierce pussy AND SO ARE YOU, 1991–2018*, a window installation at the Leslie-Lohman Museum of Art, New York.
Suffragette 2018

2019 *AND SO ARE YOU* : This iteration of the poster was produced for the spring edition of *ARTnews*.

2020 *PEOPLE HAVE THE POWER*

2022 *WE WILL HAVE WHAT WE WANT*
*Ich bin ein*e* : This poster was made for an exhibition at Between Bridges, Berlin, organized by Viktor Neumann. The translation was done in collaboration with a large cohort of German-speaking Queer friends.
we fought for the right to vote

2024 *companheiras?* : The Portuguese version of this poster was made to be exhibited alongside the original 1991 English version as a diptych. The two posters appeared in the exhibition *Queer Histories* at Museu de Arte de São Paulo, curated by Julia Bryan-Wilson and Adriano Pedrosa.

2025 *I got all my sisters with me* : This poster was conceived for *Chapter Eight* of the ongoing project *arms ache avid aeon: Nancy Brooks Brody / Joy Episalla / Zoe Leonard / Carrie Yamaoka: fierce pussy amplified*, curated by Jo-ey Tang. *Chapter Eight* took place at Participant Inc., New York. We shared the poster with multiple independent art spaces across the city to have on view and as a giveaway during the run of the exhibition.